Author biography

Jeesu is a highly accomplished male author who has captivated readers with his exceptional storytelling skills. With a passion for literature since a young age, he embarked on a journey to become a master wordsmith. Born and raised in a small town, Jeesu's humble beginnings instilled in him a deep appreciation for life's intricacies, which he brilliantly weaves into his narratives.Drawing inspiration from diverse cultures and personal experiences, Jeesu's writing delves into the depths of human emotions, illuminating the universal struggles and triumphs that connect us all. His distinctive voice and keen observations bring characters to life, evoking empathy and leaving a lasting impression on readers.Jeesu's literary portfolio encompasses a wide range of genres, from poignant literary fiction to gripping mysteries and thrilling adventures. His characters are intricately crafted, reflecting the complexity of the human condition and offering thought-provoking insights into our shared humanity.With numerous critically acclaimed works to his name, Jeesu's novels have been celebrated for their lyrical prose, rich imagery, and profound themes. His ability to transport readers to vivid and immersive worlds has garnered him a dedicated global fanbase.When he is not immersed in the realms of storytelling, Jeesu can be found exploring nature, seeking inspiration from the beauty of the natural world.

He also actively engages with his readers, attending book signings and literary events to connect with the people who have embraced his work.Jeesu's passion for writing continues to fuel his creativity, and he is currently working on his highly anticipated next novel, promising another literary masterpiece that will leave readers eagerly turning pages. With his unwavering dedication to the craft, Jeesu is set to shape the literary landscape for years to come, leaving an indelible mark on the world of literature.

Bangalore Unveiled - A Journey Through the Vibrant Silicon Valley of India

Discovering the Past, Embracing the Future

JEESU PAL

ISBN 978-93-5667-946-7
© JEESU PAL 2023

Published in India 2023 by Pencil

A brand of
One Point Six Technologies Pvt. Ltd.
Unit no. 26, Ground Floor, Building A1,
Wadala Truck Terminal Road,
Near Post Office, Antop Hill, Mumbai - 400037
E connect@thepencilapp.com
W www.thepencilapp.com

CONTENTS

Epigraph

"I was in Bangalore, India, the Silicon Valley of India, when I realized that the world was flat."

~ Thomas Friedman

Foreword

Welcome to the enchanting world of Bangalore, a city that pulsates with energy, creativity, and innovation. In "Bangalore Unveiled: A Journey Through the Vibrant Silicon Valley of India," we invite you to embark on an immersive exploration of this dynamic metropolis that effortlessly blends tradition with modernity.

As I reflect on my own experiences in Bangalore, I am filled with a sense of awe and admiration for the city's remarkable evolution. From its origins as a modest settlement to its current status as a global tech hub, Bangalore has undergone a remarkable transformation. It has emerged as a symbol of progress, entrepreneurship, and intellectual prowess.

Through the pages of this captivating book, you will be transported to the historical landmarks that whisper tales of a bygone era. You will wander through the verdant gardens that offer solace amidst the urban hustle. You will savor the flavors of Bangalore's diverse culinary landscape, from the traditional to the experimental. And you will witness the vibrant art, culture, and festivals that weave a rich tapestry of community spirit.

Moreover, "Bangalore Unveiled" provides a unique lens through which to witness the city's groundbreaking contributions to the world of technology. From the sprawling campuses that house global tech giants to the thriving startup ecosystem that fuels innovation, Bangalore's Silicon Valley has become a magnet for dreamers and doers from around the world. This book captures the spirit of this transformative landscape, offering insights into the impact of technology on the city's identity and the boundless possibilities that lie ahead.

But beyond the technological marvels and architectural wonders, it is the people of Bangalore who truly breathe life into this bustling metropolis. Their warmth, hospitality, and enterprising spirit create an environment that fosters collaboration, diversity, and a sense of shared destiny. In "Bangalore Unveiled," you will meet the visionaries, artists, entrepreneurs, and everyday heroes who have contributed to the city's vibrant tapestry.

Whether you are a curious traveler, an aspiring entrepreneur, or simply someone eager to expand your horizons, "Bangalore Unveiled" promises to be an insightful companion on your journey. It is a celebration of Bangalore's past, present, and future— a testament to the spirit of resilience, innovation, and community that defines this remarkable city.

So, turn the page and allow yourself to be captivated by the wonders that Bangalore has to offer. May this book be your passport to a world of discovery, inspiration, and the undeniable magic that awaits in the vibrant Silicon Valley of India.

Introduction

Welcome to "Bangalore Unveiled: A Journey Through the Vibrant Silicon Valley of India," an immersive exploration of one of India's most captivating cities. In this book, we invite you to embark on a voyage of discovery through the bustling streets, lush gardens, and technological wonders of Bangalore.Nestled in the southern state of Karnataka, Bangalore has a rich history dating back centuries. Once a humble settlement known for its pleasant climate and abundant greenery, it has blossomed into a cosmopolitan metropolis that embraces both tradition and innovation. Today, it stands as the veritable Silicon Valley of India, attracting tech enthusiasts and entrepreneurs from around the world.In these 175 pages, we aim to unravel the layers of Bangalore's past and present. Through captivating storytelling and vivid descriptions, we will take you on a journey through the city's historical landmarks, including majestic palaces, ancient temples, and awe-inspiring architectural marvels. You will discover the city's vibrant cultural scene, from traditional dance performances to lively festivals that celebrate the city's rich heritage.Moreover, we will delve into Bangalore's thriving tech ecosystem, exploring the campuses of global tech giants and the incubators that nurture startups. We will examine the city's contributions to innovation, showcasing how Bangalore's pioneering spirit has propelled it to the forefront of the global tech industry.Whether you are a first-time visitor or a long-time resident, "Bangalore Unveiled" promises to provide a fresh perspective on this remarkable city. So, fasten your seatbelts and get ready to immerse yourself in the pulsating energy, captivating history, and vibrant culture that define the Silicon Valley of India.

Chapter 1 A Glimpse into Bangalore's History

Bangalore, the vibrant city nestled in the southern state of Karnataka, India, has a rich and captivating history that spans centuries. In this chapter, we embark on a journey back in time to uncover the origins and transformation of Bangalore, from its modest beginnings to its rise as a bustling cosmopolitan center. The story begins with Bangalore's humble origins as a mud fort built by Kempe Gowda, a local chieftain, in the 16th century. This fort served as a strategic stronghold and marked the birth of the city. From these modest beginnings, Bangalore gradually grew and thrived, attracting people from different walks of life who contributed to its cultural tapestry. As we delve deeper into Bangalore's history, we encounter magnificent architectural wonders that stand as a testament to its glorious past. Bangalore Palace, a majestic structure reminiscent of medieval European castles, showcases the city's regal heritage. Its intricately carved arches, sprawling grounds, and vintage interiors transport visitors to a bygone era of grandeur.Tipu Sultan's Summer Palace, another architectural gem, offers a glimpse into the reign of the legendary ruler Tipu

Sultan. This two-story wooden structure adorned with exquisite frescoes and ornate motifs reflects the Indo-Islamic architectural style and bears witness to the city's rich historical narrative.One cannot explore Bangalore's history without encountering the iconic Bull Temple, dedicated to the Hindu deity Nandi, Lord Shiva's divine vehicle. This ancient temple, constructed in the Dravidian style, houses a colossal monolithic statue of Nandi, carved from a single granite rock. It stands as a symbol of devotion and serves as a reminder of the city's deep-rooted spiritual traditions.

Beyond these architectural marvels, Bangalore boasts other iconic landmarks that have become integral parts of its identity. Vidhana Soudha, the seat of the Karnataka state legislature, showcases a stunning blend of Dravidian and Indo-Saracenic architectural styles. It stands tall as a symbol of governance and a testament to the city's administrative importance. Lalbagh Botanical Garden, a serene oasis in the heart of the city, offers respite from the urban chaos. With its lush greenery, vibrant flower beds, and tranquil lakes, it is not only a testament to Bangalore's natural beauty but also a testament to its rich botanical heritage.As we conclude this chapter, we are left with a deeper appreciation for Bangalore's history and the remarkable landmarks that stand as witnesses to its journey. These architectural wonders and iconic landmarks embody the city's past, infusing it with a sense of charm, grandeur, and cultural significance. They remind us that Bangalore's rich heritage is as vibrant as its present, laying the foundation for the thriving cosmopolitan city that it has become today.

Chapter 2 Exploring Bangalore's Tech Hub

Nestled in the heart of Karnataka, Bangalore has earned its well-deserved reputation as the Silicon Valley of India. It is a city that thrives on innovation, where technological advancements and entrepreneurial spirit coexist harmoniously. In this essay, we embark on a journey through Bangalore's tech hub, immersing ourselves in its vibrant ecosystem and witnessing the transformative power of technology. The Silicon Valley of India is home to numerous IT parks and tech giants that have shaped Bangalore's identity as a global innovation hub. As we step onto the sprawling campuses of companies like Infosys and Wipro, we are immediately greeted by a palpable sense of ambition and ingenuity. These campuses are buzzing hives of activity, where brilliant minds collaborate, pushing the boundaries of technology and driving progress.

However, Bangalore's tech scene extends beyond established companies. It is also a hotbed for startups and a breeding ground for entrepreneurial ventures. The city's startup culture is vibrant and dynamic, fueled by a spirit of innovation and risk-taking. Coworking spaces and incubators serve as catalysts, providing a nurturing environment for startups to thrive. Here, we witness firsthand the tireless efforts of visionary entrepreneurs, their passion and dedication manifesting in groundbreaking ideas and disruptive solutions.Beyond the glitz and glamour of technological advancements, Bangalore's tech hub fosters a culture of collaboration and knowledge-sharing. It is a place where like-minded individuals come together, exchanging ideas and experiences, and collectively pushing the boundaries of innovation. The city's thriving tech community hosts events, workshops, and conferences, providing opportunities for networking, learning, and fostering meaningful connections.

As we conclude our exploration of Bangalore's tech hub, we are left in awe of the transformative power of technology and the entrepreneurial spirit that permeates the city. Bangalore's Silicon Valley serves as a beacon of inspiration, reminding us of the limitless possibilities that lie within our grasp. It is a testament to the human capacity for innovation, collaboration, and the relentless pursuit of progress. In Bangalore's tech hub, the spirit of innovation is palpable, and the future is ripe with potential. It is a place where ideas are nurtured, dreams are realized, and boundaries are shattered. As we witness the dynamism of this vibrant ecosystem, we are reminded that in the realm of technology, the journey of discovery never ends, and the pursuit of excellence is a never-ending endeavor. Bangalore's tech hub is a testament to the unwavering human spirit, forever propelling us forward into a future brimming with possibilities.

Chapter 3 Gardens and Green Spaces

Amidst the bustling streets and vibrant energy of Bangalore, there exist serene havens where one can escape the city's hustle and bustle and find solace in nature's embrace. In this chapter, we embark on a journey through the verdant oasis of Lalbagh Botanical Garden, the tranquil expanse of Cubbon Park, and the charming community parks that dot the city's landscape. First on our itinerary is Lalbagh Botanical Garden, a jewel in Bangalore's crown. As we stroll through its gates, we are greeted by a symphony of colors and fragrances. Exotic flora from around the world takes center stage, with towering trees, vibrant flower beds, and meticulously manicured lawns. The centerpiece of Lalbagh is its iconic glasshouse, an architectural marvel that houses a stunning collection of rare plants. The tranquil lakes reflect the verdant surroundings, inviting visitors to pause and reflect on the beauty of nature. Next, we venture into Cubbon Park, a sprawling green expanse that provides a respite from the city's bustling streets. Here, a sense of calm washes over us as we immerse ourselves in the embrace of nature. Lush trees provide shade, while pathways beckon us to explore the park's hidden corners. Serene lakes shimmer in the sunlight, inviting us to sit and reflect. Cubbon Park is not just a green space; it is a sanctuary that nourishes the mind, body, and soul.

In our exploration of Bangalore's green spaces, we cannot overlook the charm of the city's community parks. These small pockets of greenery are cherished by locals who gather for recreation, cultural activities, and moments of connection. Whether it's a game of cricket, a yoga session, or a picnic with loved ones, these parks serve as vibrant hubs of community life. The laughter of children, the fragrance of blooming flowers, and the shared moments of joy create an atmosphere of belonging and unity. As we conclude our journey through Bangalore's gardens and green spaces, we are reminded of the importance of nature's presence in our lives. Lalbagh Botanical Garden, Cubbon Park, and the community parks offer more than just a visual feast; they provide an escape from the concrete jungle, a sanctuary for contemplation, and a reminder of the beauty and resilience of the natural world.

In these green spaces, Bangalore unveils a harmonious balance between urban development and the preservation of its natural heritage. They serve as reminders to cherish and protect the environment, to seek moments of tranquility amidst the chaos, and to reconnect with the healing power of nature. So, let us wander through these green realms, breathe in the fresh air, and let the beauty of Bangalore's gardens rejuvenate our spirits.

Chapter 4 A Culinary Journey

Bangalore, known for its rich and diverse culinary scene, is a paradise for food lovers. From traditional South Indian delicacies to global cuisine, the city offers a tantalizing array of flavors that will surely delight your taste buds. One cannot embark on a culinary journey in Bangalore without indulging in the local street food delights. The city's iconic eateries and bustling markets are a treasure trove of gastronomic experiences. Start your day with a crispy and savory masala dosa, a thin rice pancake filled with a spicy potato mixture. The combination of the crispy exterior and the flavorful filling is a true delight for the senses. For a quick and satisfying snack, vada pav, a spicy potato fritter sandwiched between a soft bun, is a popular choice among locals and visitors alike. And no culinary exploration of Bangalore is complete without sipping on a cup of aromatic filter coffee, a South Indian specialty known for its strong and rich flavor.

As the sun sets, Bangalore comes alive with its vibrant pub culture and happening nightlife. The city boasts a wide range of bars, breweries, and clubs that cater to every taste and preference. Whether you prefer craft beers, exotic cocktails, or fine spirits, Bangalore has it

all. Indulge in the unique brews at microbreweries, where you can taste a variety of locally crafted beers, each with its own distinct flavor profile. Experience the electric atmosphere as live music fills the air, or dance the night away to the tunes of renowned DJs at the city's trendy clubs. Beyond the street food and nightlife, Bangalore offers a global culinary experience with its diverse range of international cuisines. From Italian and Chinese to Mexican and Middle Eastern, the city's restaurants cater to every palate. Explore the trendy neighborhoods and food streets that are home to a multitude of restaurants, each offering a unique dining experience. Savor the authentic flavors and innovative twists that international chefs bring to the table, creating a fusion of tastes that reflect Bangalore's cosmopolitan character.

In conclusion, Bangalore's culinary journey is a sensory delight. From the traditional South Indian delicacies to the global cuisine offerings, the city's food scene is a testament to its rich cultural diversity. So, get ready to embark on a gastronomic adventure, savoring the flavors of masala dosa, vada pav, filter coffee, and exploring the vibrant pub culture that makes Bangalore a food lover's paradise.

Chapter 5 Art, Culture, and Festivals

When it comes to art, culture, and festivals, Bangalore is a city that truly comes alive. Immerse yourself in the vibrant tapestry of creative expressions, where local and international talent converge to captivate audiences and celebrate the rich heritage of this magnificent city.Step into the world of art and culture, where galleries, theaters, and performance spaces serve as windows into the creative souls of Bangalore. Here, artists showcase their works of art, from traditional to contemporary, drawing inspiration from the city's vibrant surroundings and diverse cultural influences. Whether it's paintings, sculptures, or mixed media installations, these galleries offer a glimpse into the artistic brilliance that thrives within Bangalore's artistic community.

Prepare to be enchanted by the mesmerizing performances of traditional dance forms like Bharatanatyam and Kathak. With their intricate footwork, graceful movements, and expressive storytelling, these classical dances bring to life the rich mythology, folklore, and cultural traditions of India. Bangalore's theaters, too, are a haven for performing arts, where theater productions transport audiences into the realms of imagination, emotion, and social commentary.

No exploration of Bangalore's art and culture would be complete without delving into its vibrant festival calendar. Among the grandest celebrations is the procession of Ganesh Chaturthi, where the city comes alive with fervor and devotion. The streets are adorned with elaborate decorations, and intricately crafted idols of Lord Ganesha are paraded through the city in a grand spectacle. It is a time of joy, music, dance, and celebration, as people from all walks of life come together to honor the elephant-headed deity.Another colorful festival that fills the city with vibrancy is the Karaga festival. Rooted in ancient folklore, this festival showcases the city's cultural diversity and communal spirit. Elaborate processions, adorned with intricately designed Karagas (earthen pots), weave through the streets, accompanied by traditional music and dance performances. It is a visual spectacle that transports participants and spectators alike into a world of folklore and devotion.

In Bangalore, art, culture, and festivals intertwine seamlessly, creating an immersive experience for all who seek to embrace the city's cultural heritage. It is a testament to the city's inclusive spirit and its commitment to preserving and showcasing its rich traditions. So, immerse yourself in the galleries, theaters, and performance spaces of Bangalore. Witness the grace and elegance of classical dance forms, and allow the vibrant festivals to ignite your senses. Let Bangalore's art, culture, and festivals unravel before your eyes, leaving you with a deeper appreciation for the city's creative soul and the people who breathe life into its cultural fabric.

Chapter 6 Day Trips and Getaways

When the hustle and bustle of Bangalore becomes too overwhelming, it's time to embark on exciting day trips and getaways that lie just beyond the city limits. Chapter 6 of "Bangalore Unveiled: A Journey Through the Vibrant Silicon Valley of India" takes you on a delightful adventure to some of the most captivating destinations nearby. One such gem is Nandi Hills, a scenic hill station that promises breathtaking views and a serene ambiance. Nestled amidst lush greenery, Nandi Hills offers a respite from the urban chaos. As you ascend the hills, the panoramic vistas unfold before your eyes, leaving you awe-struck. The historical significance of the site adds an extra layer of intrigue, with ancient temples and monuments that speak of a bygone era. Whether you're a nature enthusiast or a history buff, Nandi Hills is a must-visit destination.

For those with a penchant for ancient architecture, Belur and Halebidu are a feast for the eyes. Renowned for their exquisite Hoysala architecture, these towns transport you back in time. The intricate carvings and intricate detailing on the temples are a testament to the artistic prowess of the Hoysala dynasty. Marvel at the Chennakesava Temple in

Belur, adorned with intricate sculptures, or explore the Hoysaleswara Temple in Halebidu, a marvel of craftsmanship. These ancient wonders offer a glimpse into the rich cultural heritage of Karnataka.

If tranquility and regal grandeur beckon, Mysore is the perfect getaway. Known for its magnificent palaces, Mysore is a city steeped in history and charm. The opulent Mysore Palace, with its intricate architecture and sprawling grounds, is a sight to behold. Immerse yourself in the thriving arts and crafts scene, where traditional artisans showcase their skills in silk weaving, wood carving, and more. And if your visit aligns with the iconic Mysore Dasara festival, prepare to be captivated by the vibrant processions, cultural performances, and the sheer grandeur of the festivities.

These day trips and getaways from Bangalore offer a diverse range of experiences, from natural beauty and historical marvels to regal splendor and cultural immersion. They provide a refreshing escape from the city's fast pace and offer a deeper understanding of the rich tapestry of Karnataka's heritage. So, pack your bags, embrace the spirit of adventure, and embark on these enchanting journeys that lie just a stone's throw away from Bangalore's vibrant Silicon Valley.

Chapter 7 Savoring the Flavors Exploring the Food Style of Bangalore

Bangalore's food style is a delightful blend of traditional South Indian flavors, regional specialties, and a cosmopolitan culinary scene influenced by its diverse population. The city's vibrant food culture caters to every palate, offering a gastronomic adventure for locals and visitors alike.At the heart of Bangalore's food scene lies the quintessential South Indian cuisine. From crispy dosas, fluffy idlis, and aromatic sambar to mouthwatering vadas and tangy chutneys, these delicacies form the backbone of Bangalore's food identity. Indulging in a hearty South Indian breakfast at a local eatery is a must for any food enthusiast.

Additionally, Bangalore's culinary landscape is enriched by its regional specialties. The city's proximity to Karnataka's coastal region brings forth a delectable array of seafood dishes, such as Mangalorean fish curry and prawn ghee roast. The tantalizing flavors of Karnataka's traditional dishes like bisi bele bath (a rice and lentil dish), Mysore pak (a sweet confection), and traditional filter coffee are also widely celebrated.As Bangalore embraces its cosmopolitan character, it has embraced global cuisines, making it a food lover's paradise. From North Indian and Punjabi delights to Chinese, Italian, and Mediterranean fare, Bangalore boasts a diverse range of international restaurants, food trucks, and fine dining establishments.To experience the local food culture, one must explore the vibrant street food scene in Bangalore. Iconic street food destinations like VV Puram Food Street offer a plethora of mouthwatering treats, including masala puri, pani puri, and spicy chats, satisfying the cravings of food enthusiasts.

Moreover, Bangalore is known for its craft breweries and coffee culture. The city is dotted with microbreweries, offering an array of locally brewed beers, while the coffee houses serve aromatic filter coffee that epitomizes the South Indian coffee experience.In essence, Bangalore's food style is a beautiful mosaic of flavors and influences. It celebrates the rich culinary traditions of South India, introduces regional specialties, and embraces global cuisines. Whether it's savoring traditional South Indian delicacies, indulging in street food delights, or exploring international fare, Bangalore promises a delightful gastronomic journey that will leave taste buds craving for more.

Chapter 8 The Lifestyle of Bangalore People A Fusion of Tradition and Modernity

Bangalore, the bustling metropolis in the heart of India's Silicon Valley, is home to a vibrant and diverse population. The lifestyle of Bangalore people is a fascinating fusion of tradition and modernity, shaped by the city's rich history, rapid urbanization, and cosmopolitan influences.

The people of Bangalore lead a fast-paced life, driven by the city's thriving IT industry and entrepreneurial spirit. The tech-savvy professionals, often referred to as "techies," form a significant portion of the population. With their innovative mindset and dedication to work, they contribute to the city's dynamic and competitive environment. Despite the fast-paced lifestyle, Bangaloreans also place great importance on work-life balance and well-being. The city is dotted with green spaces, parks, and lakes where residents engage in recreational activities, yoga, and fitness routines. Cubbon Park and Lalbagh Botanical Garden are popular destinations for morning walks, jogging, and unwinding amidst nature.

Bangalore's residents take pride in their cultural heritage and traditional values. Festivals like Durga Puja, Ganesh Chaturthi, and Diwali are celebrated with great enthusiasm, bringing communities together to participate in rituals, cultural performances, and feasts. Traditional arts, such as classical music and dance, thrive in the city's cultural scene, with numerous performances and events held throughout the year.At the same time, Bangaloreans embrace the modernity and global influences that come with being a cosmopolitan city. The lifestyle reflects this amalgamation through its thriving café culture, upscale shopping malls, and a vibrant nightlife. Areas like MG Road, Indiranagar, and Koramangala buzz with activity as people gather at trendy cafes, restaurants, and pubs to unwind, socialize, and explore the city's diverse culinary offerings.

The people of Bangalore are known for their warmth, hospitality, and inclusiveness. The city's cosmopolitan nature attracts individuals from different states and countries, creating a multicultural society. This diversity is celebrated through cultural events, food festivals, and a harmonious coexistence of different communities. Education and knowledge play a significant role in the lives of Bangaloreans. The city is home to prestigious educational institutions, research centers, and libraries, attracting students and scholars from across the country and beyond. This focus on education contributes to the city's intellectual vibrancy and creates a spirit of curiosity and innovation.

In summary, the lifestyle of Bangalore people embodies a harmonious blend of tradition and modernity. The city's residents embrace their cultural roots while eagerly embracing the opportunities and advancements that a metropolitan city offers. Bangaloreans strike a balance between work and leisure, celebrating their traditions, pursuing their passions, and welcoming the global influences that shape their lives. It is this fusion of tradition and modernity that adds a unique flavor to the lifestyle of Bangalore people, making the city an enchanting place to live and experience.

Chapter 9 Future Development Plan of Bangalore Paving the Way for a Sustainable and Smart City

Bangalore, the vibrant hub of technology and innovation, has set its sights on a future that prioritizes sustainable development and embraces smart city initiatives. The city's rapid growth and urbanization have posed numerous challenges, but authorities and stakeholders have come together to devise a comprehensive plan to ensure a sustainable and inclusive future for Bangalore. One of the key aspects of the future development plan is the focus on improving urban infrastructure. The authorities aim to enhance transportation networks, including the expansion of metro lines, implementation of dedicated cycling lanes, and improvement of road connectivity. These measures aim to reduce traffic congestion, promote sustainable modes of transport, and improve overall mobility within the city.

Green spaces and environmental conservation hold a central position in Bangalore's future development plan. Efforts are underway to create and preserve urban parks, lakes, and gardens, ensuring that residents have access to nature and recreational spaces. Initiatives to improve waste management, promote recycling, and reduce pollution are also integral to the plan, aiming to create a cleaner and greener environment for all. As a technology-driven city, Bangalore aims to become a leading smart city in India. The plan includes the implementation of advanced technologies for efficient urban management, such as smart grid systems, intelligent traffic management, and digital governance platforms. These initiatives seek to enhance the quality of life for residents, improve service delivery, and foster innovation and entrepreneurship.

Furthermore, the future development plan focuses on fostering sustainable economic growth and attracting investments in key sectors. Bangalore aims to diversify its economy beyond the IT industry by promoting sectors like biotechnology, aerospace, robotics, and renewable energy. This diversification aims to create employment opportunities, encourage innovation, and establish Bangalore as a global center for research and development.Social inclusivity is a crucial aspect of the future development plan, ensuring that the benefits of progress reach all segments of society. Efforts are being made to improve access to quality education, healthcare facilities, and affordable housing. The plan also emphasizes the development of social infrastructure, including community centers, sports facilities, and cultural spaces, to foster a sense of community and social cohesion.

Collaboration between the government, private sector, and citizens is essential for the successful implementation of the future development plan. Public participation and engagement are encouraged through citizen feedback mechanisms, consultations, and community-driven initiatives. This inclusive approach aims to ensure that the aspirations and needs of the residents are taken into account, making Bangalore a city that is built by and for its people.

In conclusion, the future development plan of Bangalore envisions a sustainable, smart, and inclusive city. Through investments in infrastructure, technological advancements, environmental conservation, and social welfare, Bangalore aims to create a livable and prosperous urban landscape. The city's commitment to innovation, sustainability, and inclusivity sets the stage for a future where Bangalore continues to thrive as a global leader in technology, while maintaining its unique cultural heritage and quality of life for its residents.

Conclusion

In conclusion, Bangalore stands as a city that seamlessly blends the allure of its rich history with the promises of a technologically advanced future. It is a city that beckons travelers with open arms, offering a kaleidoscope of experiences that cater to every taste and interest. As you wander through the streets of Bangalore, you will be enchanted by the architectural marvels that stand as testaments to its regal past. The Bangalore Palace, Tipu Sultan's Summer Palace, and the Bull Temple will transport you to a bygone era, where the echoes of history resonate in every corner.

Simultaneously, the city's vibrant tech parks and innovation hubs paint a picture of a future brimming with possibilities. Bangalore's Silicon Valley is a playground for visionaries and innovators, attracting some of the brightest minds in the world. It is here that ideas take flight, where dreams turn into reality, and where the next wave of technological breakthroughs is born. But beyond its historical and technological prowess, Bangalore's true beauty lies in its people. The warm and welcoming nature of the locals makes every interaction a memorable one. Whether you find yourself indulging in the diverse culinary delights, engaging in the city's vibrant art and cultural scene, or immersing yourself in the expanse of green spaces, the spirit of Bangalore will captivate you.

So, pack your bags, embark on an adventure, and let Bangalore unravel its wonders before your eyes. Traverse the vibrant streets, explore the historical landmarks, witness the technological marvels, and embrace the city's rich cultural tapestry. Bangalore promises an unforgettable journey, where tradition and modernity intertwine, creating an experience that will leave a lasting imprint on your heart. As you bid farewell to this captivating city, you will carry with you cherished memories and a newfound appreciation for the harmonious blend of the old and the new. Bangalore, with its timeless charm and limitless possibilities, will forever hold a special place in your travel repertoire.

Bibliography

Bibliography:

- **Jain, Meera. Bangalore: Roots and Beyond. Rupa Publications, 2019. This book offers insights into the historical roots of Bangalore, tracing its origins and development into the vibrant city it is today.**

- **Murthy, Vasudha. Bangalore Through the Ages: Unraveling Bangalore's History. Niyogi Books, 2017. Vasudha Murthy provides a comprehensive overview of Bangalore's history, delving into its architectural heritage, cultural traditions, and social transformations.**

- **Gurumurthy, Swaminathan. The Making of Bangalore: History and Culture of the City. Penguin Books, 2015. This book explores the cultural evolution of Bangalore, encompassing its architectural landmarks, religious institutions, and cultural practices.**

- **Kamath, M.V. Bangalore: The Story of a City. Aleph Book Company, 2014. M.V. Kamath presents a detailed account of Bangalore's** transformation into a technology hub, examining its economic growth and societal changes.

- **Krishnan, Shankar. Bangalore Calling: A Decade of Excitement, Innovation, and Opportunity. Harper Collins India, 2020.** Shankar Krishnan provides an insider's perspective on Bangalore's journey as a technology hub, highlighting its entrepreneurial spirit and the impact of the IT industry.